空手道
Karate
Made Simple

2 Punching, Kicking, and Blocking

Maiko Nakashima
with the Japan Karate Federation

The Oliver Press, Inc.
Minneapolis

INTRODUCTION

Karate-do is a Japanese *budo*, or martial art. It originated on the Japanese island of Okinawa and spread to the rest of Japan. *Budo* is a part of Japanese culture that is based on traditional combat skills. Like all forms of martial arts, the goal of karate is not just to defeat your opponent; it is also to discipline heart, mind, and body through practice and respect for one's opponents.

Karate-do, or the "way of karate," is now known around the world as "karate." In 2010, the World Karate Federation (WKF) had members in 187 countries, and estimates that around 50 million people study karate. Every two years, there is an international tournament, the World Karate Championships, in which athletes gather from all over the world to compete.

By reading this book, you will be able to answer these questions:

- **How do you form a fist?**
- **What does "No aggression" mean?**
- **How many stances are there in karate?**

Recently, there has been a movement in Japan to place more importance on traditional Japanese culture, including karate. Starting in 2012, all middle-school students were required to take a *budo* class. Imagine being required to take karate as a gym class!

This series is divided into four books that will introduce you to karate in an easy-to-understand way.

In this series, you will learn how this martial art spread from a small island to become a worldwide phenomenon.

CONTENTS

Stances

It is important to learn the proper stances from the start in order to deliver powerful and accurate punches or kicks.

Various stances

In karate, there are dozens of stances. In this book, we introduce thirteen main stances. "Foundational stance" is the most common stance in sparring. The others are needed while practicing forms (see p. 24).

Here, using "closed foot stance" as an example, we show the points that are common to all stances.

● Closed foot stance

Stand with feet together. Be erect but not stiff.

Look straight ahead.

Pull chin back.

Be careful not to tense neck and shoulders.

Keep center line of the body straight.

Keep *tanden* as your center of the body (see text box).

Knees are slightly bent, not locked.

● Formal attention stance

Bring heels together, with toes one fist's width apart. This stance is used while bowing.

● Parallel stance

Feet are shoulder width apart. Lines from little toes to heel on both feet must be parallel.

● Natural stance

Feet are shoulder width apart as in parallel stance. Toes point out in a natural position.

Tanden

Open ready position

The part of the body just under the navel is called the *tanden*. It corresponds to your center of gravity. Keeping centered on your *tanden* enables you to be stable and react quickly at any time in karate.

4

Naihanchi stance (ship riding stance)

Legs are further apart than parallel stance. Toes point inward.

Imagine flexing thighs inward.

Horse stance

Wider distance between feet than parallel stance. Lines from little toe to heel on both feet must be parallel.

Be careful not to bend knees inward.

Square stance

Distance between feet is almost the same as horse stance. Toes point outward. Lower your hips.

Be careful not to bend knees inward.

Hourglass stance

Feet are shoulder width apart. Toes point inward. Flex toes to grip the floor.

Front heel and back toe are on the same line.

Basic stance

Feet are shoulder width apart. Leading foot is a comfortable distance forward. Back foot points out in a natural position.

Put weight on each leg equally.

Front stance

Leading foot is farther forward than in basic stance. Bend front knee deeply, but keep front knee behind the front foot.

Be careful not to bend knees inward.

Don't lift the heel.

Back stance

Spread feet apart. Bend one knee and put your weight on it. Look back over opposite shoulder.

Stances can differ slightly from one style to the next, even when they're called the same name.

Side-facing back stance

Open legs wide and bend one knee deeper than back stance. Toes on the other foot point forward.

Keep knee bent.

Cat stance

Bend back knee deeply and put most of your weight on it. Lift front heel.

Keep straight.

Weapons of the hand and body

The whole body can be a weapon in karate. Here we show parts of the body used most often to attack.

Characteristics of karate techniques

Karate is a weaponless martial art. The "weapons" are the hands, feet, arms, legs, and even head. The same part of the body can be used in multiple ways. For example, the hand can be used to chop, punch, or gouge, depending on how the hand is positioned.

Karate movements are not simply a matter of moving your legs or arms. For example, a front punch gains its power by rotating the hips and shoulders to throw the arm forward.

What is meant by "no contact"?

In most karate competitions, full contact blows are prohibited. The ability to stop at the moment of contact takes great skill and control.

It is important to learn how to deliver the techniques powerfully in an appropriate way in training, rather than merely knowing what they are.

On the next page, we will introduce how different parts of the body are used in karate.

Full contact blows are usually not allowed in competition.

● Weapons of the body

Arm		
Fist	Back fist	Hammer fist
Knifehand	Ridgehand	Spearhand
Palm heel	Elbow	Forearm
Leg		
Ball of foot	Foot edge	Instep
Heel	Knee	

Only the most common striking techniques are introduced here.

Fist

The basic shape of the hand in karate is the fist. The hand should be curled tightly, but not clenched, so that it will not collapse under impact. The name of a strike depends on which part of your fist is used for striking.

⌐ ¬ Area to use for attack.

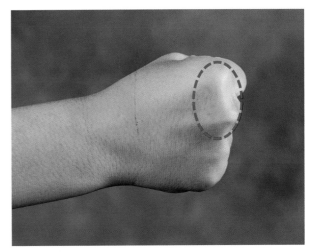

● **Back fist**

Strike with the back part of the knuckles. Most frequently used to attack the face or side of the body.

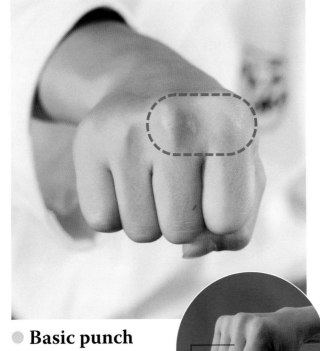

● **Basic punch**

Strike with the first two knuckles of the fist. Most frequently used in sparring and forms.

Make four fingers flat.

● **Hammer fist**

Hold fist vertically and swing as you do with a hammer.

How to make a fist

Bend your fingers one by one starting from the little finger. Fold fingers tightly into the palm and bend the thumb over them. Make fist tight but not clenched. The tip of the thumb should not stick out.

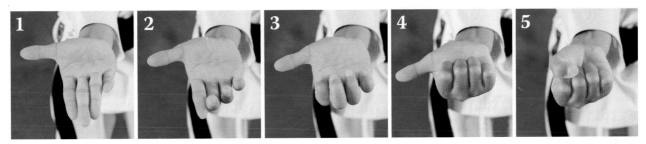

Other hand techniques

There are ways to use the hand as a weapon besides making a fist.

● **Knifehand** Align four fingers and bend the thumb tight against them. Hand resembles the shape of a sword. Use the little finger side to attack vulnerable areas such as the neck.

● **Ridgehand** Align the fingers and bend your thumb tight like for a knifehand attack. Strike with the joint of the thumb.

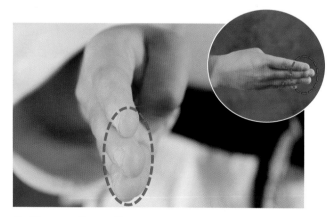

● **Spearhand** Align four fingers and strike with fingertips. Be careful not to allow fingertips to separate or bend back. This is a strike that can break the fingers and should not be done without intense conditioning.

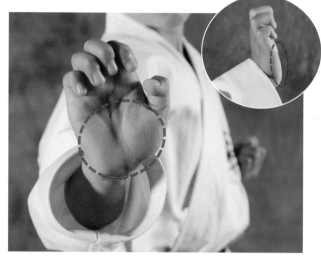

● **Palm heel** Bend the hand perpendicular to the wrist and curl the fingers. Use the lower part of the palm to attack opponent's nose, chin, or abdomen.

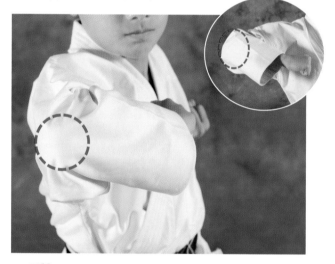

● **Elbow** Bend the elbow and strike with the point. Use to attack at close range.

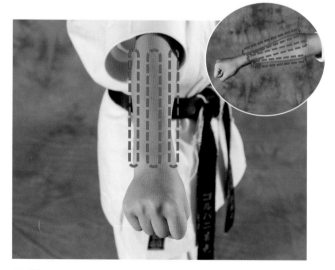

● **Forearm** The part of the arm from elbow to wrist is called the forearm. It is used to block the opponent's attack.

Foot attacks

Though not as versatile as the hand, various parts of the foot are used to attack the opponent.

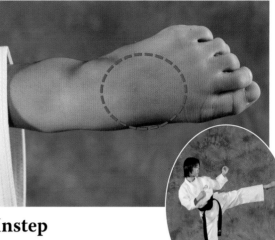

Instep

Point your foot and strike with the instep, or top, of the foot. Toes should be pointed. This is often used for a roundhouse kick.

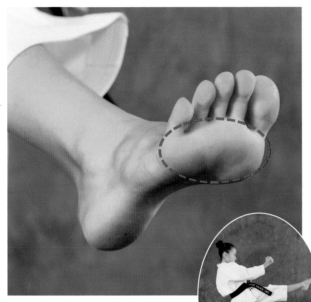

Ball of the foot

Point your foot and pull the toes back. This is often used for a front kick.

Heel

Flex your foot toward your knee and hit with the heel. It is used when the opponent is behind you.

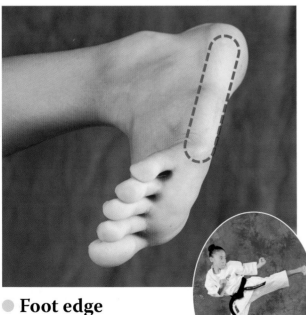

Foot edge

Bend your ankle inward and flex foot toward knee. Bend the toes back. Use the outer edge of your foot to attack the opponent.

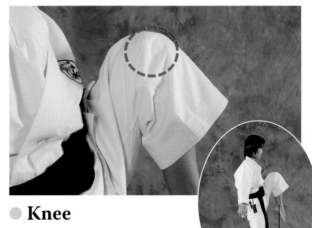

Knee

Lift knee to strike, keeping your leg as close to your body as you can. Point foot up when attacking and down when defending.

3

Punches

Karate techniques include punching, striking, blocking, and kicking. First let's examine punches. Punches attack opponents with a fist or other hand position in a straight line.

Basic punch

Punching with the hand on the same side as the foot that steps forward is called a "front punch." A punch with the opposite hand is called a "reverse punch."

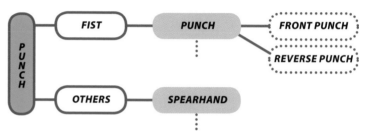

HAND POSITION: FIST

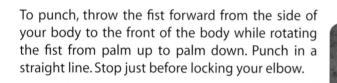

Punch

To punch, throw the fist forward from the side of your body to the front of the body while rotating the fist from palm up to palm down. Punch in a straight line. Stop just before locking your elbow.

BAD EXAMPLE

- Look straight forward.
- Pull chin back.
- Keep elbow close to body.
- Opposite hand makes a fist on the side under the armpit.

Extend arm at chest height.

Don't bend wrist up and down or sideways.

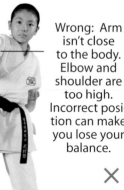

Wrong: Arm isn't close to the body. Elbow and shoulder are too high. Incorrect position can make you lose your balance.

✕

Bend knees a little bit. Be careful not to extend fully.

Keep center of the body straight.

10

Front punch

Stand in front stance (see page 5). Use the hand on the same side as your front foot. You can deliver the punch from a standing position or step forward as you throw the punch.

Don't pull back the shoulder of your opposite hand.

Punch at chest height.

Opposite hand should make a fist on the side under the armpit.

Reverse punch

Stand in front stance. Use the hand opposite from your leading foot. A reverse punch has more power than a front punch because of the greater motion, but you must be closer to strike.

Punch at chest height.

Punch while rotating the hips. This motion creates a powerful strike.

Don't lift the heel.   Keep knee behind the toes.

Don't lift the heel.   Keep knee behind the toes.

Spearhand

The spearhand is used to attack an opponent's eyes or throat with your fingers.* Because it requires intense conditioning to prevent injury, it is mainly used in *kata* (see page 24). Just like a reverse punch, striking while rotating the hips creates more power.

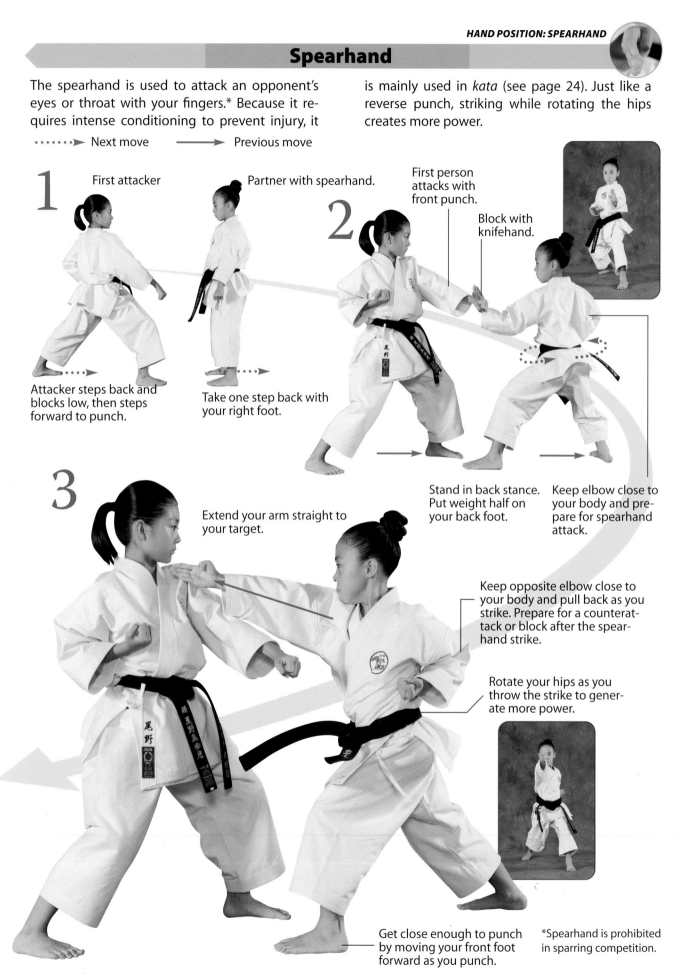

······▶ Next move   ⟶ Previous move

1 First attacker   Partner with spearhand.

Attacker steps back and blocks low, then steps forward to punch.

Take one step back with your right foot.

2 First person attacks with front punch.

Block with knifehand.

Stand in back stance. Put weight half on your back foot.

Keep elbow close to your body and prepare for spearhand attack.

3 Extend your arm straight to your target.

Keep opposite elbow close to your body and pull back as you strike. Prepare for a counterattack or block after the spearhand strike.

Rotate your hips as you throw the strike to generate more power.

Get close enough to punch by moving your front foot forward as you punch.

*Spearhand is prohibited in sparring competition.

12

Strikes

While punching techniques attack the opponent straight on, hand strikes come from multiple angles and use a variety of hand positions.

How are strikes used differently from punches?

In sparring, most attacks are punches that are thrown straight out from the body. Strikes can come from many directions, and are more common in *kata* (see pages 24 – 28). Here we show three main striking techniques.

1 Assume ready position.
2 Person on the right blocks the attack from the person on the left.
3 Person on the right counterattacks with a strike.

HAND POSITION: KNIFEHAND

Knifehand strike

The knifehand strike is used to attack the side of your opponent's neck by moving your hand in a half circle from outside.

First person prepares to attack.

Partner stands in open ready position.

1

Prepare to step back with your right foot.

······▶ Next move
——▶ Previous move

2 Begin attack with front punch.

Block with forearm.

Swing hand around in a half-circle with the palm facing up.

Keep elbow close to your body and pull chin back.

3

Keep elbow close to body and prepared to strike.

Don't lift the heel.

Step forward with leading foot as you strike.

Ridgehand strike

Like the knifehand strike, the ridgehand strikes the opponent's neck by moving the hand wide from outside.

••••••▶ Next move   ──────▶ Previous move

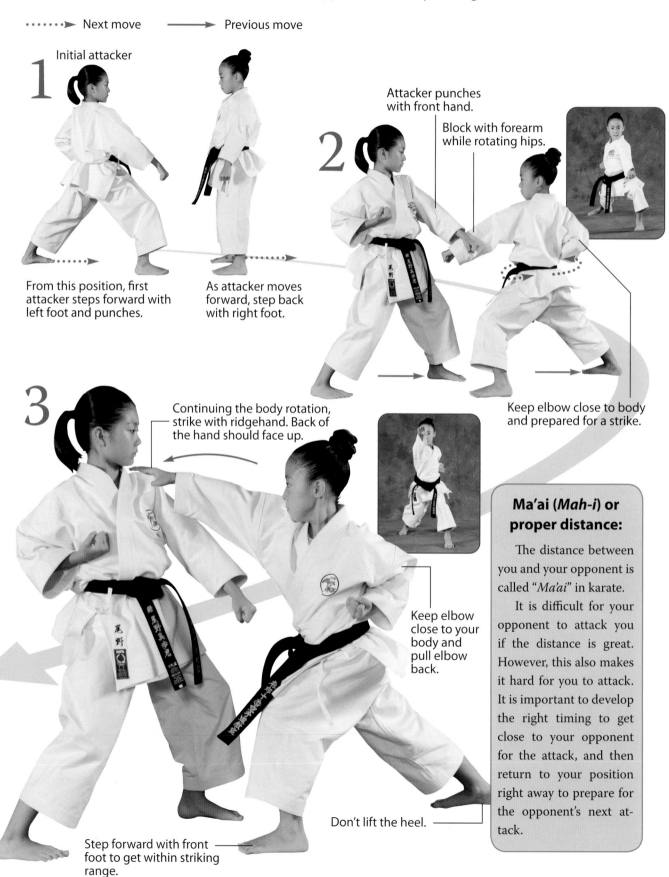

1 Initial attacker

From this position, first attacker steps forward with left foot and punches.

As attacker moves forward, step back with right foot.

2 Attacker punches with front hand.

Block with forearm while rotating hips.

Keep elbow close to body and prepared for a strike.

3 Continuing the body rotation, strike with ridgehand. Back of the hand should face up.

Keep elbow close to your body and pull elbow back.

Don't lift the heel.

Step forward with front foot to get within striking range.

Ma'ai (*Mah-i*) or proper distance:

The distance between you and your opponent is called "*Ma'ai*" in karate.

It is difficult for your opponent to attack you if the distance is great. However, this also makes it hard for you to attack. It is important to develop the right timing to get close to your opponent for the attack, and then return to your position right away to prepare for the opponent's next attack.

Hammer fist strike

A hammer fist can be used in several different ways to attack your opponent. It can hammer down from above your head or attack the ribs by swinging sideways.

1 Initial attacker

Partner with hammer fist strike

Take one step forward.

Take one step back.

2 Front hand punch

Block with forearm

Keep elbow close to your body and pull elbow back.

Pull right foot back into a cat stance while pulling right fist back to your ear.

3 Bend elbow.

Shift weight onto left foot. Raise fist.

4 Hammer down with your fist by extending your arm.

Keep elbow close to your body and pull elbow back.

Step forward with front foot to close the distance.

15

Kicks

Kicking techniques can cause more damage than punches or strikes because of their greater power. Here we show four common types of kicks.

Supporting foot is more important than kicking foot

It is important to keep your balance while kicking. If you are off-balance, your kick will be weak and it is more likely that your opponent will attack you.

1 Balance yourself.
2 Pull kicking leg close to your body.
3 Kick. 4 Pull your leg back.
5 Return to initial position.

STRIKING SURFACE: BALL OF THE FOOT

Front kick

The most basic kicking technique is the front kick. This kick generates power by thrusting forward with your hip as the leg is extended. It is most often used to attack your opponent's midsection.

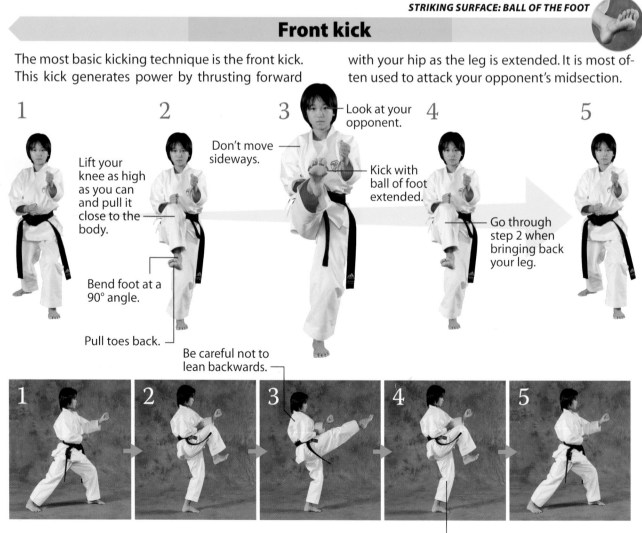

1

2

3 — Look at your opponent.

Don't move sideways.

Lift your knee as high as you can and pull it close to the body.

Bend foot at a 90° angle.

Pull toes back.

Kick with ball of foot extended.

4

5

Go through step 2 when bringing back your leg.

Be careful not to lean backwards.

1   2   3   4   5

Balance by bending the supporting leg.

Side kick

When doing a side kick, it is very important to keep the body upright and balanced. The side kick is used to strike your opponent's head, midsection or lower body, such as knee joints.

1 Ready position

2 Bend your foot inward so the edge is ready to strike.

Lift your knee as high as you can and pull it close to the body.

3 Look at your opponent.

Kick using the edge of the foot.

4 Go through step 2 when bringing back your leg.

5

High • Middle • Low Techniques

In karate, body targets are divided into three areas:

Head, neck → High

Chest, abdomen → Midsection

Lower abdomen, knees → Low

High side kick

Supporting foot rotates as kick is thrown.

Keep center of the body straight while kicking.

17

Roundhouse kick

The roundhouse kick is a little more difficult because it can be hard to keep your balance. The key is to lift your foot as high as your knee in step 2.

The roundhouse kick can be aimed at any target, but is usually directed at the upper or middle part of the opponent's body.

······▶ Next move   ⟶ Previous move

1

Pull knee up and back.

2

3

Foot is pointed to strike with instep.

Go back to step 2 when bringing back your leg.

4

5

Extend leg while turning your hips.

Balance your body by slightly bending the supporting leg.

Foot turns while kicking.

High roundhouse kick

Flex ankle.

Be careful not to lower the knee while kicking.

1   **2**   **3**   **4**   **5**

Lift your knee only as high as you can lift your foot.

18

Back kick

The back kick is effective for catching your opponent off guard. It is an advanced technique, however, as it requires you to turn your back on your opponent.

1

2

Look at your opponent.

Pull heel to buttocks.

Rotate in a half circle and put weight on your front foot.

Heel up and toes down.

3

Look over your shoulder while kicking straight out.

4

● Back kick to midsection.

Balance your body by slightly bending your supporting leg.

Pull leg back and return to your initial position.

1 **2** **3** **4**

Hips should stay in one place even while leaning back and kicking.

6

Blocks

Blocking techniques are specific ways to defend yourself from an attack. They stop an attack rather than dodging or avoiding it.

Match your block to the attack.

The blocking technique to use depends on the opponent's attack. Here we show the four main types of blocks.

1 Assume ready position.
2 Person on the right blocks the attack from the person on the left.

BLOCKING SURFACE: FOREARM

Rising block

Upper rising block is used when the opponent attempts to punch at head level. It is crucial to thrust your arm all the way above your head quickly.

Next move
·············▶

Previous move
──────▶

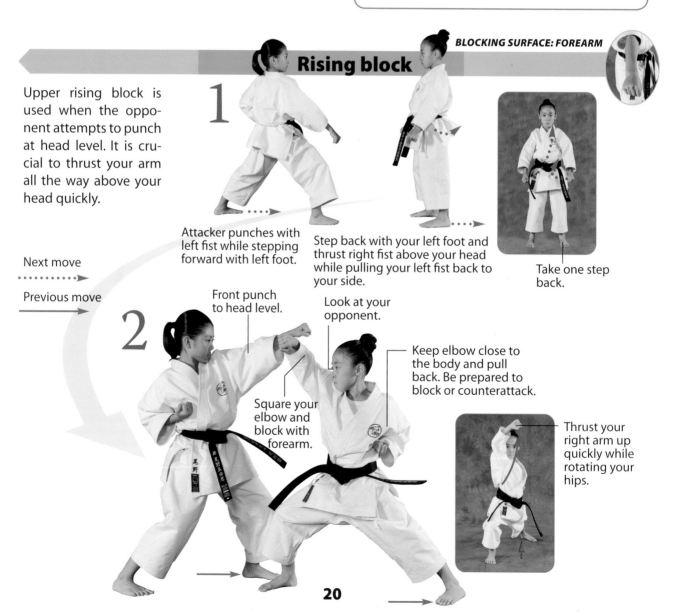

1

Attacker punches with left fist while stepping forward with left foot.

Step back with your left foot and thrust right fist above your head while pulling your left fist back to your side.

Take one step back.

2

Front punch to head level.

Square your elbow and block with forearm.

Look at your opponent.

Keep elbow close to the body and pull back. Be prepared to block or counterattack.

Thrust your right arm up quickly while rotating your hips.

20

Inside forearm block

An inside forearm block is used when the opponent attempts to attack your midsection. It is important to keep your center of gravity low so you don't lose your balance.

1

Attacker prepares by stepping back with the left leg and blocking low with the right hand.

Take one step back.

Take one step back with your left foot. While turning the hip, bend your right elbow as you raise your fist. Bring your left fist back to your side.

Swing your flexed right arm horizontally across the front of your body.

2

Attacker punches with left fist while stepping forward with the left foot.

Keep left elbow close to the body and pull fist back. Prepare for the next block or counterattack.

Step firmly forward to block.

DID YOU KNOW?

What does "no aggression" mean in karate?

Karate is a spiritual discipline, not just a physical one. It was primarily developed as a form of self-defense. It should never be used to start a fight. At the same time, blocking can be very effective against an opponent by stopping an attack when it is being thrown full force. In this sense, a blocking technique is not all that different from an attack.

21

Outside forearm block

Just like the inside block, the outside block is used when the opponent punches toward your midsection. Move your arm quickly to the outside. Be careful not to lose your balance.

······▸ Next move   ⟶ Previous move

1

Attacker prepares by stepping back with the left leg and blocking low with the right hand.

Take one step back.

Step back with your left foot and swing right fist up as if you were drawing a circle around your elbow. At the same time, rotate your hips to the right. Bring your left fist back to your side.

2

Move arm as if drawing a circle around your elbow.

Look at your opponent.

Attacker punches with left fist while stepping forward with the left foot.

Keep elbow close to your body and pull fist back. Prepare for the next block or counterattack.

22

Sweeping (low) block

The sweeping block is used for low or midsection attacks. Step back diagonally as you raise your hand and then block with a downward sweeping motion.

1

Attacker lifts rear foot while shifting weight to the front foot.

Lift up.

Take one step back.

Step back diagonally with your left foot and raise your right fist to your left shoulder.

2

Look at the opponent.

Front kick to the midsection.

Keep left elbow close to the body and pull back. Prepare for the next block or counterattack.

Weight is still on your right foot.

23

7

Kata (practice forms)

A series of defending and attacking movements performed against imaginary opponents in a set pattern is called kata, *or forms.* Kata *allow you to combine all elements of movement, including stance, speed, and timing.*

Characteristics of *kata* (forms)

Kata were originally developed as a way to practice without a partner. They are a good way to improve, since they contain a variety of techniques. In forms, the sequence of movements is set. It can be helpful to imagine using the techniques against opponents. Forms follow a variety of floor patterns. The movements may make the shape of a T or the letter 工.

Kata in competition

The *kata* competition is an important part of karate tournaments that demonstrates accuracy, power, and speed.*

Each karate style has different forms. There are over a hundred different *kata*, spread across different styles. In tournaments organized by the Japan Karate Federation, only certain forms called "specified forms" are allowed. These include selected forms from each karate style.

*Details of *kata* competition are introduced in book 3.

● These *kata* are internationally understood by the Chinese names.

School name	Goju	Shotokan	Shito	Wado
1st specified forms	Saifa, Sepai	Jion, Kankudai	Bassai-dai, Seienchin	Seishan, Chinto
2nd specified forms	Sesan, Kururunfa	Enbi, Kankusho	Matsumura rohai, Nipaipo	Kushanku, Niseishi
Selected forms	Seiyunchin, Shisochin, Suparinpei, etc.	Tekki-shodan, Jitte, Shisochin, etc.	Jitte, Jion, Jiin, Matsukaze, Wanshu, Suparinpei, etc.	Naihanchi, Bassai, Rohai, etc.

Saifa   Sepai   Jion   Kankudai   Bassaidai   Seienchin   Seishan   Chinto

Kata: Sepai

One of the characteristics of Sepai is its circular movement. There are a number of movements in which one blocks the opponent's attack and simultaneously counterattacks. The key is to perform each movement crisply.

······▶ Next move ——▶ Previous move

● Main move

4TH movement

Focus on the opponent.

8TH movement

Right hand on top and and left hand underneath, with palms facing each other (Heaven and Earth position).

Ki-yaah!

Sweep your right foot one time and position yourself into square stance. Distance between legs should be a little narrow. Make fists with both hands and pull them up to your armpits. Punch down as you stomp with the right foot.

Square stance (see page 5)

Backs of the hand are facing out.

13TH movement

Strike your opponent.

Block your opponent's attack.

Next movement is to turn by rotating both feet.

Drop your hips.

Turning cross-leg stance

(The above pictures show part of each movement.)

DID YOU KNOW?
When I use Japanese words, how do I make them plural?

The Japanese language is different from English because it doesn't really have plural words. If you are using a Japanese word in English, the proper way would be to say "two *dojo*" or "two *kata*" instead of adding an "s." However, when foreign words become part of the English language, they are often treated like any other English word. So don't be surprised if you hear someone talking about learning their "*katas*" instead of "*kata.*"

Kata: **Kankudai**

Kankudai has the greatest number of movements among the first group of specified forms. It is constructed for all kinds of imaginary attacks. Movements such as jump kicks or dropping to the floor are the main characteristics of this form.

········► Next move

──────► Previous move

◆ Main move

4TH movement

Block opponent's attack.

Raise hands slowly, with right hand on top.

1ST → 2ND → 3RD movement

Right palm facing up and left palm facing right side.

Turn palm upward and pause. Bring side of hand to chest.

Natural stance (see page 4)

Slowly.

Turn hands out. Bring down as you make a circle.

Quickly!

16TH movement

Block your opponent's attack.

Back fist vertical round strike

Side round knifehand strike

Front stance

Pull up your leg as you jump.

Strike as you go into front stance.

Pull your leg high and jump into the air to execute double kick.

63RD → 64TH → 65th movement

Land in front stance.

Front stance

(The above pictures show part of each movement.)

26

Kata: Seienchin

Seienchin is used when the opponent is at very close quarters. The same movements are delivered repeatedly. Although there are many movements in this form, there are no kicking techniques.

◆ Main move

Lift up both open hands slowly as if you are scooping. Put back of your hands together in front of the chest.

Square stance (see page 5)

Slowly.

3ʳᵈ → 4ᵗʰ → 5ᵗʰ movement

Downward block.

Do not move hips up and down.

Block the opponent's attack with knifehand block.

Back of the hand faces down in front of the solar plexus.

Stay in square stance.

Turn over your hand to hook the opponent's punch (hook block).

Block your opponent's punch with lower part of your palm.

Cat stance with right foot in front. (see page 5)

Lift up your right elbow to the height of your shoulder.

50ᵗʰ → 51ˢᵗ movement

Strike with back fist as you move forward.

① ②

Stay in cat stance. Use wave movement* to move your front foot forward. Back foot slides forward.
*Wave foot: Move forward by sliding your foot on the floor, heel to toes. The movement is similar to a wave.

Last movement

Square your elbows.

Square your elbows.

Make mountain shape with both hands.

Cat stance with left foot in front.

(The above pictures are one part of each motion.)

27

Kata: Chinto

Chinto has fewer movements than most *kata*; however, there are many different types of stances and most of them require quick movements. It is important to watch your balance as your weight will shift frequently depending on the stance.

◆ Main move

1ST movement

Right palm faces outside, left palm faces towards you.

Block together with right and left hand.

Fold in both thumbs.

Thigh is flexed inward.

15TH movement

Shoulder and hip should be parallel to the floor.

Bend knees and shift weight. Lean the center of your body back.

Stand in side-facing back stance while extending the left knee.

Bend knees in same direction as your toes.

24TH movement

Lift left foot to avoid a sweep attack. Front part of the left foot should slightly touch the knee.

Kick with the ball of the foot.

Bend knees slightly. Be careful not to lose your balance.

(The above pictures show one part of each movement.)

What is "practical application of forms"?

Each form has a meaning. Demonstrating each movement with an opponent is called "practical application of forms."

Understanding the significance of forms

Each movement in a *kata* is directed toward an imaginary opponent. Those who perform *kata* should understand the meaning of each move as if fighting an actual adversary. "Practical application" is a method to show whether one understands how the techniques can be used. When done with a partner at advanced competitions, the skillful performance of these drills demonstrates the application with enormous intensity.

"Practical application" makes it easy for spectators to understand the meaning of forms. You can always hear the crowd cheering whenever the performance of application starts.

INDEX

GLOSSARY

Japanese Transliteration	Pronunciation	Meaning
Budo	*Boo-doe*	Martial arts
-dachi	*- dah-chee*	- stance
Kata	*Kah-tah*	Forms
Karatedo	*Kah-rah-teh-doe*	Way of Karate
Ma'ai	*Mah-i*	Distance
Naihanchi	*Nye-hahn-chee*	Ship-riding (stance)
Tachikata	*Tah-chee-kah-tah*	Stances
Tanden	*Tan-den*	Center of gravity

Schools	Pronunciation
Goju	*Goh-jyu*
Shito	*She-toe*
Shotokan	*Show-toe-kan*
Wado	*Wah-doe*

WEBSITES

Karate World:
http://www.karatedo.co.jp/index3.htm

World Karate Federation:
http://www.wkf.net/index.php

Japan Karatedo Federation:
http://www.karatedo.co.jp/jkf/jkf-eng/e_index.htm

This edition published in 2013 by The Oliver Press, Inc.
Charlotte Square
5707 West 36th Street
Minneapolis, MN 55416-2510

KARATE MADE SIMPLE: PUNCHING, KICKING, AND BLOCKING

Original Japanese title: KIHON WO KIWAMERU! KARATEDO: TACHIKATA/ WAZA/ KATA
(Mastering the Basics! Karatedo: Stances, Techniques, and Forms)
© Champ Co., Ltd., 2011
All rights reserved.
Original Japanese edition published in 2011 by Champ Co., Ltd.
English translation rights with Imajinsha Co., Ltd. through Japan UNI Agency, Inc., Tokyo

Library of Congress Cataloging-in-Publication Data

Nakashima, Maiko.
Karate made simple 2 : punching, kicking and blocking / Maiko Nakashima with the Japan Karate Federation.
    p. cm. -- (Karate made simple)
Includes bibliographical references and index.
ISBN 978-1-934545-18-8
1. Karate--Juvenile literature. I. Title.
GV1114.3.N36 2012
796.815'3--dc23
                        2012033029

Text: Maiko Nakashima with the Japan Karate Federation
Translation: Chiaki Hasegawa and Goldie Gibbs
U.S. editing: April Stern
U.S. production: Clay Schotzko

Picture Credits:
All images courtesy of Champ Co., Ltd. and Imajinsha Co., Ltd.

ISBN: 978-1-934545-18-8
Printed in the United States of America
17 16 15 14 13   8 7 6 5 4 3 2 1